CW01163517

ICONIC

ICONIC

SERAPHINA WILDE

CONTENTS

1 Introduction to Iconic Celebrities — 1
2 Early Life and Background — 3
3 Rise to Fame — 5
4 Challenges and Setbacks — 7
5 Achievements and Milestones — 9
6 Impact and Legacy — 11
7 Personal Life and Relationships — 13
8 Philanthropy and Activism — 15
9 Evolution of Public Image — 17
10 Media and Public Perception — 19
11 Transition to Other Platforms — 21
12 Exploration of Different Genres — 23
13 Collaborations and Partnerships — 25
14 Behind-the-Scenes Insights — 27
15 Mentorship and Influence — 31
16 Iconic Moments and Memorable Events — 33
17 Fanbase and Fandom Culture — 35

18	Global Reach and International Appeal	39
19	Criticism and Controversies	41
20	Adaptations and Reinterpretations	43
21	Iconic Fashion and Style	45
22	Iconic Quotes and Catchphrases	49
23	Iconic Roles and Characters	51
24	Iconic Performances and Productions	53
25	Iconic Songs and Albums	55
26	Iconic Films and TV Shows	57
27	Iconic Artistic Collaborations	59
28	Iconic Business Ventures	61
29	Iconic Awards and Recognitions	63
30	Iconic Endorsements and Sponsorships	65
31	Iconic Social Media Presence	67
32	Iconic Fan Interactions	69
33	Iconic Charity Events and Initiatives	71
34	Iconic Achievements in Sport	73
35	Iconic Achievements in Science and Innovation	75
36	Iconic Achievements in Politics and Leadership	77
37	Iconic Achievements in Literature and Writing	79
38	Iconic Achievements in Music and Performing Arts	81
39	Iconic Achievements in Visual Arts and Design	83
40	Iconic Achievements in Film and Television	85

41	Iconic Achievements in Fashion and Beauty	87
42	Iconic Achievements in Business and Entrepreneursh	89
43	Iconic Achievements in Philanthropy and Social Imp	91

Copyright © 2024 by Seraphina Wilde
All rights reserved. No part of this book may be reproduced in any manner whatsoever without written permission except in the case of brief quotations embodied in critical articles and reviews.
First Printing, 2024

CHAPTER 1

Introduction to Iconic Celebrities

Key image and reality attributes of iconic celebrities, how they are scrutinized, and their media are the focus of this book. Fourteen women and men who have at least fifty years of celebrity are examined via their careers, as celebrities, and as individuals. Although sensationalized by their public myths, they, like all other people, are ordinary human beings who are subjected to the same vulnerabilities as the rest of us. Far too often, they are scapegoats paraded to the public in filling the age-old mythic function of purification through confession and punishment. The purpose here is to look beyond the images and to gain some understanding of who they are as people and how they perceive themselves. Why are we curious about these iconic celebrities and their incredible journeys?

The book finishes with some surprises. The celebrities never expected to be as successful as they are, and it comes as a shock to them. By a large majority, they never went seeking the fame of which they ended up as celebrities, and they would frequently give back the fame and fortune if given the opportunity to re-choose in their lives. Comments throughout the book illuminate this, and what exactly are the differences the subjects perceive between themselves and "everybody else." Consideration is given to the public's definition of celebrity in the celebrities' own terms. Because the research is based on an objectivism standpoint, much use is made of celebrities' own words. This approach respects celebrities' advanced level of self-awareness, and it is designed to lead the reader to think critically, not to dismiss the book's findings as biased.

CHAPTER 2

Early Life and Background

John Fitzgerald Kennedy was born in a wealthy, politically ambitious family, which had established a place for themselves in America's social and intellectual elite. They had been in the country since 1847, with a background mainly Black-Irish, while on his mother's side his blood showed two highly influential American families—the Fitzgeralds and the Bennedicts. These bloodlines stretched all the way back to the very foundation of American society and brought in a piece of American history to contrast with the immigrant past of his paternal ancestors. It was on one side a past that engendered pride and a sense of destiny and on the other a sense of struggle, of being a part of the struggle of the minority to assert their place within a society dominated by its Anglo-Saxon origins.

His family was very much a family who looked to the past and were intensely conscious of the importance of their heritage, a family who epitomized the American Dream of wealth, success, and social position. They projected a united front to the outside world, complete with recognized status symbols such as leisure and service industries to attend to their every need at their various homes—Hyannis Port, Edgartown, Palm Beach, and Georgetown.

These outward symbols ensured respect and esteem as America's own royal family—that is, as seen from the outside, by those not close enough to see the personality clashes and family feuds which did exist.

She walked a fine line through all these family squabbles and divided loyalties because she led all her life the life of a woman who battle-hardened by adversity. The man in the hallowed center of her life for declining fortunes was Joseph Kennedy.

CHAPTER 3

Rise to Fame

The year 1913 was a crucial turning point in Charlie Chaplin's career. By the time he made The New Janitor at the end of that year, which features him in a supporting role as a character called "Stick" and was directed by his friend Carl Harnick, he was on the verge of greatness. According to his recently hired research associate, David Robinson, The New Janitor was the key factor that persuaded Mack Sennett to take him on. Sennett may have been particularly sensitive to Chaplin's fateful aura and potential status, as indicated by his incredulity at the depth of public concern at the prospect of Chaplin leaving Sennett less than two months after his arrival at the Keystone Studio. However, by that time the public, with the help of filmgoers, other films, and a fast-expanding national press, was already celebrating his triumphs in and interpreting his comic routines of double-takes, proscenium-like framing of wise-cracking moral mayhem, Jack-in-the-Box-like leaps onto passing streetcars, and purported exploding glitter-dust of pure energy and incongruity.

When the comedies appeared at the beginning of 1914 at the rate of one or two Chaplin films a week he remained on the top. In fact, contrary to popular perception, he continued to be the top dog in 1915, a year when he received more press attention than any other actor except William S. Hart, the box-office and critical sensation of the moment. He also was the first of all Comique players to become an international phenomenon. By 1915, Enrico Tosi, an Italian journalist who visited America, discovered that its theaters had three idols, William S. Robert Dickson found his films showing in the smallest hamlets and biggest cities of India, and an American correspondent misunderstood an Austrian movie magnate who had paid more than a quarter of a million dollars for the European rights to a comedy.

CHAPTER 4

Challenges and Setbacks

Journeying toward iconic status encompasses dramatic swings. At times, individuals, one day heroes, are defined as zeroes the very next day. Experiencing such disappointment does humble some, making them more human and often enables them to become celebrities possessing hearts. Also, logging a one-way ticket as zeroes are the peripheral celebrities who gradually fade to the other side of the moon. Still, it is the seismic shifts in celebritydom that capture attention and compel one to realize that journeys taken, but not completed, often times haunt us far worse than the journeys never begun. Finally, not attaining iconic status often allows the aborted to reside in a comfort zone that those defining the future are forever relinquishing.

We must not forget the heavy prices that we all sometimes have to pay for being in the public eye. Media scrutiny often probes too deeply into one's private life. Potential presidential candidates and actual presidents are asked questions that one should not inquire about in polite company. Privacy invasions are also rampant in the lives of personalities who falsely believe that they are friends with the world, only to find that their innermost secrets are tabloid fodder. After a positive or negative evaluation of the famous is made, it is often overemphasized as isolated instances are seldom forgotten and tend to last for a lifetime. This is an added burden.

CHAPTER 5

Achievements and Milestones

It is amazing how many astonishing achievements these remarkable men and women have managed to rack up. For instance, Mohammad Ali has reigned as boxing's heavyweight champion more times for more years than any other person. While he won the Olympic middleweight boxing title long ago, in a kind of twilight victory, the subsequent medal at the prestigious international film festival at Venice can't have anything second-class about it. Marilyn Monroe has been voted the number one sex star year after year. In her short life, she made a major impact on talking pictures, lifting herself to the rank of an amazing comedienne, one who has kept a whole generation laughing through sheer stamina but who, above all, remains an unforgettable sex idol in an age when some of the films made only twenty-five years ago have already sunk into oblivion.

Sean Connery was caught once and for all in the net of the 007 film-public love affair throughout the world for years. And yet, in fact, he has been the best-known interpreter of the Bond roles for only three years (1965-68). But there must be dozens of other film views among the blockbusters invented by producer Albert Broccoli;

yet none have been taken to heart as this one has. I must confess, the esteem John Lennon has been experiencing these past few years strikes me as truly extraordinary. We're not just talking about a gifted songwriter who has led various bands to runaway success, but also a dramatist and film actor who captivated critics, without straining to improve his technique, and has been elected to play the leading role in more than a film a year for the last decade... and continues not to let himself be caught.

CHAPTER 6

Impact and Legacy

Legacy, for those who have lived fruitful lives, is the foundation upon which we build the future. Despite obscurity during their lifetimes, many celebrities continue in perpetuity to influence the many aspects of public life with which they were involved during their stay in the fast lane. Their legacies occupy an iconic place in the public relations and institutional memory of their home countries. Singers such as Elvis Presley, John Lennon, and Jim Morrison are extraordinary phenomena who continue to attract attention more than a generation after they left the stage. The word 'iconic' favours the specific and the immediate, the stopping power of elites and their entourages, the ongoing ability to surprise and delight, and a refreshing countenance despite the reins of time.

The human face that emerges as iconic over time seems to retain characteristics that very selectively identify it as a masterpiece. The same layered detail and vivid expression marking art seems to be potentially present in the person. This sculpturing of the human experience into a clear, unifying event is solely the work of society. Collectively and individually, we choose blemishes as well as fairy tale memories that our collective actions attach to extraordinary celebrities. There is no perfect or readily imaginable institutional arrangement or market that could devise public faces as enigmatic and emotionally charged by their absence as by their omnipresence. Celebrity institutions can merely foster the growth of channel capacity, but success as an iconic form of life is up to artist and public. Celebrity historians make the final choice regarding who or what will someday join the elite ranks of the iconic. Ordinary public figures can be facilitated, encouraged, promoted or hidden from view, but the ultimate product that emerges from the global gallery is solely a manifestation of the interest of the participating public.

CHAPTER 7

Personal Life and Relationships

The eighth chapter of Iconic explores the personal lives and relationships of twenty celebrities. Their segues into romance, marriage, and family have led them to further self-actualization, personal rewards, heartaches, and drama. Many celebrities share their personal lives, always very judiciously and with the caveat that nobody really knows what goes on behind closed doors except the couple in question. Our twenty celebrities are no different. Seven are married, two are divorced, four are in long-term relationships, and seven are single. Some have children, others are childless at this point in their lives. Most do not have the luxury of privacy. All live in self-imposed prisoners of themselves, knowing that anything that they say, write, or post may influence popular culture. Distorting communication rhythms leads to distorted lives.

Some media outlets often envision perfect family vignettes, relying on selective, almost 100% inaccurate portrayals of coupledom and the stories that come with it. Compelling personal characteristics of a few relationships: longevity, relationships that have been ongoing but are not marital; high-profile relationships that only heightened a celebrity's profile; and success or potential career killers, all with the inherent pressures of a high profile, were legendary editors expunged columns filled with personal prurience of most minor celebs and turned them into major celebrities. It should be noted that in the last year, four media outlets merged; only one that took over a magazine had any real investment in celebrity relationships. With white whales, coupled with too good to be true success stories that all blend into a hodgepodge, partners must find reasons to love and be loved – leaving many stuck in relationships of convenience. Celebrity love stories (and often, the endings of those love affairs) can fit the narrative, but last a week. With the exception of granny rags, articles follow the Madonna e-whore cypher which shills product, but never covers lives cluttered with mindfully, loving, considerations to neglect.

CHAPTER 8

Philanthropy and Activism

A number of the individuals profiled in this book have parlayed their wealth, fame, and influence into foundations and charitable work. The reasons for this are as varied as the individuals themselves. Steve Martin is an established collector of fine art who some years ago accepted an invitation to serve on the Board of the Los Angeles County Museum of Art. Martin's volunteer efforts at LACMA included the co-curation of a major exhibition, Picasso and Portraiture: Representation and Identity, for which he garnered acclaim for his fresh insights and thoughtful remarks. As his familiarity with the museum world gradually grew, so too did his appreciation for the many ways in which museums serve their communities. Steve Martin's dream is to build a world-class museum to house his extensive collection of fine art. It is to this end that he created the Steve Martin Charitable Foundation. The Foundation, through its grants, directly advances the dual goals of expanding the creative potential of artists and of reaching, exciting, and engaging the broadest possible public. The Foundation exists as the embodiment of Steve Martin's wish to benefit the public as well as to fulfill and share his ideal of what a museum and its functions might be.

Sir Elton John possesses a vast collection of modern and contemporary photography, largely of the photographic representation of social concerns and human conditions. Away from the public's view, Sir Elton has also been deeply engaged in the challenge of raising awareness of gender issues in South Africa, particularly as regards women and girls infected and affected by HIV/AIDS. In dire need of changes to policies and funding, Sir Elton started to give serious consideration to the ways in which his art collection could be used to complement his ongoing philanthropy work. These efforts came to fruition when he established the Elton John AIDS Foundation's Photography Portfolio produced and curated by the renowned gallerist, Daniel Wolf. Walt Disney was a genius who brought joy to millions through his characters and his theme parks. He was also known for acting upon his absolute conviction that, with imagination and hard work, one can make the world a better place. Since 1927, one year after the release of the first Mickey Mouse animation, Walt's company has been actively involved in supporting children's social, educational, and medical care, vital community rebuilding efforts and environmental change. Disney, its talented employees, and fellow volunteers serve with excellence and distinction in promoting vibrant economies; building stronger, healthier communities; and making transformative changes around the globe. Contributions to worthy causes are not only made from corporate profits, but include individual gifts and charitable sponsorships. The Walt Disney Company has a long and cherished tradition of giving back to the communities in which its employees live and work. The success of each, in various ways, is indicative of the incentive good fortune might create in its beneficiaries.

CHAPTER 9

Evolution of Public Image

The overwhelming majority of iconic celebrities are confronted with an unwelcome double-bind. They are public figures, and they have public images. Few people who become celebrities know what a public image is before they are offered large sums of money to become actors, musicians, models, or athletes; they become celebrities by performing and selling their talent (usually to established celebrities). As part of their livelihood, they must face judgment, gossip, and speculation about which they ordinarily, and sometimes raucously, would have a right to tell the world to buzz off. Their employers - studio, team, record company, or personal manager - demand no less than from their employees, and they exact severe penalties if they decline. On the contrary, the organization in charge of their living condition - committees, wielding pens, cameras, and eyeglasses - design the public image of their staff and spend even more time criticizing their personnel's supposed flaws.

Iconic celebrities have been around seemingly forever and are engaged in work that involves little or no ethical or intellectual effort, interests a large portion of the public at the same time, and still has no direct effect, such as emergency care for the ill in Guatemala, mobilizing the citizen into public debate about taxes, family policy, or the environment. The participants are not without skills; to make sports or rock stars benefits a few people. Not everyone can do it. They need coaching, training, skills, tutors, and wheels; they can be leaders, self-confident, and creative. But the most memorable moments of typical working days take up the task of self-exposure to demonstrate apparent skills that have no positive contribution to achieving desirable social goals. Such actors, however skillful, primarily act in a public, not a private, capacity. Public respect, and other employment obligations, are the foundation of the celebrity's public image; it is a calculated role and reputation rather than neurotic jeopardy.

CHAPTER 10

Media and Public Perception

The men and women who appear before us on the screen or stage perform an unusual kind of magic. They create memorable public images. For the most part, we meet them in their conspicuous moments or in dramatic association with the events of our lives. The characters they portray become, in the minds of millions, a model for a doctor or an idea for a politician. To the impressionable fan, Errol Flynn is Robin Hood. Walter Brennan is the western prospector. Frank Morgan is the wizard of Oz. And logically enough, Greta Garbo is just as she appears in Camille, reluctantly quitting a life of sumptuous misery or, possibly, browsing in a New York delicatessen.

It is ironic, then, that celebrities are so seldom taken as they choose to project themselves on and off the screen or stage. Hedda Hopper's renowned collection of testimonials about Miss Garbo was the result not of a press announcement the actress held, but of Miss Garbo's first public appearance in 44 months to greet her friend, the Paris smog. After the familiar massive build-up, Frank Sinatra's allegedly duffer, revolver-packing, girl-pursuing, effete-forsaking image was shattered by the Phrygian-capped bobby-sox army who wept lugubriously before the barricades. Fans could not have coaxed bigger box office returns by straining-timorously, of course- to get a glimpse behind the scenes at Mr. Sinatra's meetings with Martin Bormann.

CHAPTER 11

Transition to Other Platforms

Television takes time, and although its rewards are substantial, being on television can open up other, quicker, more congenial fields to explore. The big talent agency and the big stars realize that television is the ultimate way to project an image. The sky is the limit; presidents, popes, and primates will make their debut on television, and not for any personal promotion, but for their causes and messages. The medium can make or break you, and for a host of undeniably gifted stars, it has made them stars of a slightly diminished wattage.

My father listened to the fights and the wild, seemingly impossible broadcast performances Stepin Fetchit put together, and always remembered him as being wonderful. There is no doubt that Stepin did things no other actor could do, but his choice of material, and the color of his skin, made him a star of a completely different magnitude from the one that finally developed. At four years old, I got my first pair of boots, and the bar of soap with its inscription of Kings Of The West; after dinner, we would sit in father's sumptuous chairs, lace up my boots, and erase the inscription, telling tales of ancient and glorious western triumphs. The silence in which none of us mentioned him no doubt brought relief to my father.

CHAPTER 12

Exploration of Different Genres

Amir's recent album, "Access of Admitance," was intensively promoted both by clubs and the biggest pop-music festival in Russia, and even by the Kremlin. This was a follow-up to his victory at a musical talent contest in which leading Russian music producers took part as the jury. The victory gave Amir a chance to embody his dream, like in a fairytale. Amir was born into a Jewish family in the Dagestani town of Derbent. The word "Amir" is translated as "the Prince" from Arabic and has an Israeli pronunciation. He studies at a Jewish secondary school. However, it is hardly visible in his outward appearance. His amiable and humorous lyrics are liked by the girls, some of whom are much older than he is. The gang and producers have brought the music video for Amir's song from Paris, which was made especially for the school. On Thursday evening, the show received very high TV ratings, and the Song television channel was happy to broadcast Amir's show the following weekend after the contest. Indeed, the show is worth broadcasting, which can be explained by the band of young but cool instrumentalists, the dance group Luxa (made at Premax school), and the paparazzi and show business photographers. The Discovery-Music team says that the producer and impresario Igor Krutten sees a real star soulster in Amir. Amir himself says, "OK, it's a secret of Popular."

CHAPTER 13

Collaborations and Partnerships

Under the Influence garnered other opportunities for affiliated partnerships. One came from the internet provider America Online (AOL), which in the late 1990s was experiencing a decline in customers. Norton Interactive Media sent HipPop to the parent company of AOL. AOL responded positively and agreed to host the HipPop website, present advertisements in the web-videos, and offer HipPop-sponsored classes. These collaborations attracted back a portion of AOL's lost customer base of 2.8 million, which made AOL a happy company. Monetarily, everything was looking fine. But already our zeal for HipPop had been waning despite the successful launch and profits. So, we took the money generated and left AOL a little confused about what we were supposedly doing with our subjects of influence.

The underpinnings of our underwhelming feelings were threefold. One, the HipPop class offerings on AOL prefaced that of ventures by celebrities—such as Apollo, where various forms of training had always been a part of the package. My relationship with Norton Interactive Media had already been problematic. The "hip" design and scripted language drew up a social contract I was not willing to keep—especially with my race. Even HipPop's success and $300,000 offer to expand were not sufficient to compensate for the negative psychic balance. Hence, the decision was made to stop production.

CHAPTER 14

Behind-the-Scenes Insights

This book has pointed out numerous traits that are common to many true superstars, while offering many techniques that enable readers to be more like an exceptional leader. By mastering millions of decisions, better choices can be made throughout the day, just like a superstar leads and inspires thousands, hundreds, or dozens of devoted and determined workers. The accomplishments of a Yoda, Skywalker, Spurrier, or Larry Bird are due to their doing millions of things better every day. These incredible outcomes are no accident. With the insights shared in this book, it is now so much easier to learn from these exceptional people and to create their kinds of amazing results.

Former Notre Dame University coaching legend Lou Holtz once wisely proclaimed, "talent is God-given, so be humble, and fame is man-given, so be thankful." For people who have been blessed with exceptional amounts of these scarce resources, it is always worthwhile to explore at least in part their journey to greatness. The journeys of Barbie, Betty Boop, Spock, Taylor, Tarzan, Wanda, Beethoven, Yoda, and hundreds of similar household names were each quite different, but contain a number of common characteristics. Understanding how these uniquely talented people succeeded in their quest can make it so much easier to learn from their many remarkable experiences. By discovering how these unique, historic personages established their greatness, how their tragedies shattered their dreams (Barney, Pooh), and how they overcame their enormous challenges (Miss Piggy), we can not only understand better how these uncommon celebrities earned their unique status, but also learn how we can improve our personal and professional lives. By modeling ourselves after these remarkable people, just as we model ourselves after a grandfather, chairman of the business, or a parent, we can teach ourselves how to succeed while learning from the experiences of these famous leaders reshaping and sharpening our role.

Understanding how a Yoda achieved supreme success and how to avoid the mistakes made by celebrities hold valuable insights that are invaluable. Are the steps needed to reach our goals. Since so many of today's best-known companies, public agencies, sports, theatrical, and musical acts, celebrities, and admired persona ha formed a vision and carefully planned their path in ways noteworthy and predictable, it is enlightening to explore briefly a few of these many fascinating stories to learn about their mission, values, strategies, inno both Lrs, technologies, culture, and many lessons learned. The complexity of the challenges of reaching and retaining these top-performing statuses is often underestimated and misunderstood by onlookers—but can be simplified by just learning from the documented journeys of extra uniquely talented celebrities that most everyone instinctively recognizes as being unique. Few people may possess the talent to be a realistic Skywalker, Barbie, or Da Vinci, but at least it is possible to know what is needed to help realistic people succeed, and what is required to avoid some of the most noted mistakes made by those who have universally failed. While business and life may be misunderstood, it is timely to pay homage to what is considered to be of paramount importance to everyone who has experienced the magical moments and injustices that are shown in front of all of us, everyone can learn and profit by exploring the extraordinary journeys of these amazing, remarkable, talented individuals.

CHAPTER 15

Mentorship and Influence

One important part of reflecting upon your early achievements is looking back to evaluate who mentored and influenced you in order to become who you are. Mentorship develops within a social context. Research has revealed how African American school students were able to acquire cultural knowledge not taught by the teacher by mentoring and dialoguing with each other about their responses to problematic school contexts. Powerful mentoring and influence develop within the context of role modeling both in public, and often even more significantly, through involvement in specialized communities where general influence is not the goal. This ability to guide and influence is often taken in very different ways by different mentors and heroes. Personal growth, much like learning, is never a zero-sum game. Greatness is not something that diminishes when it is given. Failure to recognize the benefits and joys of both influence and influence on the paths of your friends may ensure that recognition never comes your way.

Consequently, it is scandalous to watch people refuse to idealize their mentors and friends within the fields of popular celebrity. When people idealize public figures, they don't hold the idealization exactly. This is why being able to distinguish, to reverence, and to love is such an important part of being able to construct a sensible critique. Allowing enduring heroes to fade from public consciousness can be a pernicious action. The terrain of popular culture offers such incredible potential. If it is only a force that people use against you, then all of your exploitation fears are well justified. We need models of what human life as artful practice might look like. If you were ever mentored, we need to raise the stakes of your legend and teach its moments to emerging stars. Part of ensuring that this is a world that makes sense is providing the broadest range of heroes. The fact remains that almost any public successful person who is told by an aspiring child that they're a hero knows this: more than any single deific representation of a mortal within our entire culture, the mortal who lived up to this abuse entrusts that impression with a truth that they themselves would not maintain. Celebrity-be what you are valued as being. Become tremendous.

CHAPTER 16

Iconic Moments and Memorable Events

Everyone who achieves the status of a legend has a set of memories that go with the acclaim. Those moments of acclaim may be recognition, the clamor of the public, or the cheers of the multitude. They vary from celebrity to celebrity, but they carry the indelible mark of exceptional prowess, the pursuit of success with virtually monomaniacal purpose. They are when the competitive thrust attains sublime exhilaration with its concomitant rewards. The celebrity basks in that very warmth of fame.

A fleeting moment of fame, but usually not very sustainable. The fickleness of celebrity usually outlives the intensity of acclaim. Few celebrities manage it better than for a short term, and the vast majority have a briefer moment of basking in the limelight than they expected. The demands of a spoiled public quickly turn into "What more; what else can you show us that is different?" as if the original vision has not gone on to scramble for something else more, better, and fresher.

CHAPTER 17

Fanbase and Fandom Culture

Why People Follow Celebrities: The Attraction of Fame and Power

Why are people so eager to follow celebrities? It seems that celebrity news and gossip have become more and more popular in recent years. It is always shocking to hear, for example, debates about the Bubble Gum Crisis during the broadcasting of an evening news program. Celebrities retain the power to make headlines on television and in print. Entertainment media has become the people's main source of news and education. TV programs can turn even the most controversial political issue into a joke, providing easy-to-swallow infotainment for the masses. In the meantime, hard-hitting news reports cannot compare in terms of their ratings. In addition, reality TV programs remain the most watched by TV viewers. The exhibitionistic actions of ordinary people like those in reality programs enchant the public imagination. There is little else. It is fair to say that the entertainment media has deeply affected the thoughts, attitudes, and fates of the public.

What value do celebrities hold for society? In addition to entertainment, do celebrities provide any other service for society? Although this seems to be a mysterious question, we can conclude that the main attraction celebrities hold for their audience is first fame, or the power to gain attention and awe from the public. The social and identity components of fame offer us so much about whom we are and where we stand. The wave of celebrities that have entered the consciousness of public life over the last two decades have much in common. They represent a palpable shift in the nature of stardom and how people process stardom. At the beginning of the new millennium, the qualities of fame and celebrity have changed. People celebrate as esteemed celebrities the individuals – performers, artists, writers, scientists, and politicians – who work within the mass mediascape, the celebrated.

The transformation of the media and the cult of the individual "force" celebrity upon a weary populous. It is something distinctly less charismatic and of a lesser order. Besides talent – real, exaggerated, or non-existent – not simply with being famous, but with having presentational skills above those from other professionals. The complete media saturation of this new mass-mediated parade marries this peculiarly modern brand of fame with the technological communications that feed it. In their knowledge of the media world and the control that they exercise, these celebrities represent an essential embodiment of the power behind their own status. For many people in the media industries, these newly formed players in the 'economic, political, cultural, and technological communities' of the global society are no longer seen as celebrities, but as an emergent form of technocratic elite: the celebrated. Other successful specialists who do not wield the same influence are much more ambivalent in their relationships with or recognition of their celebrated status. This contemporary worship only takes a little stepping back to become unmasked rebellion. A few exposed frames of its pedestal: and the illusions are immediately shattered into the dust of kitsch. Fandom and debates about it demand discursive defense. The spectacle remains, the fascination lives on. Celebrity, popularity, and fame have also gained even more prestige.

CHAPTER 18

Global Reach and International Appeal

Madonna, every step of the way, has been a Gulliver in about as Latino, as French, as British - to say nothing of a New York or L.A.-y way as it is possible to be. Her noted sardonic and rapier spiking on practically any given subject makes the movies a dialogue in a self-deprecating way reminiscent of, and perhaps even supplied by, its brothers-in-arms, the British music halls. The movies are also largely a vehicle (sweet chariot) for supporting contributors made famous by Michael Jackson videos, whose blockbusters clarify how such flash also has substance: In essence, a seamless blend of song, dance, and dialectic that grows up and develops, scene by scene, in such a way as to make lighter and, dare one render the pun less than, the media. They might have been made for television. They are television worldwide and as rare as left-handed compliments. To vanquish a quotable quote of Music Corporation of America forecasting Vice President Sidney Binsabaums: "She is more exciting to more people in more countries than Sly Stallone and Bill Cosby combined."

CHAPTER 19

Criticism and Controversies

The high price tag of celebrity residencies also sends a pusillanimous message to the repertory and chamber music communities – promoting a situation in which young musicians can see themselves as true success stories only by working in the shadow of the international highly paid megawatt pop-classic star. I quoted the examples of Audra McDonald, Lea Salonga, and Barbra Streisand who finished young in grade A Broadway musical theater and transferred intact to the world of opera – adding some versatility by taking on a few sudden film and sitcom projects (the Whoopi Goldberg example now updated to a more classical model for other reasons) and I referred to the instance of Delia Reese. Granted that pimp is a harsh word, for a professional in residence of such extreme glamorous star casting with the widest consideration and humanity including even less-renowned but higher-real-earning contemporary models might introduce a query that is more disturbing.

Existing jet-set flight paths might also be scrutinized, taking off from operatic and symphonic centers in Zurich, Berlin, London, Paris, and New York only to land in San Francisco, Chicago, and Los Angeles – stopping off in Edinburgh and Melbourne to pick up the star composer of a "street-wise" opera, possibly linked in audience appeal to that special power to sell known by a few actors from film and TV, etc., and possibly featuring a role written for their voice: the performer in residence as principal spark? And in New York is there really a need for the operatic passion plays of both "deep south" and "far east", where a quiet parachuting for the displaced heartland seems in order in order that the great migration north can proceed? Casual speculations aside, the matter of improving conditions does need to be tackled.

CHAPTER 20

Adaptations and Reinterpretations

At the end of the twentieth century, Death of a Salesman continued to be performed. Despite the incalculable distance separating Willy from the celebrities, his anguish still found resonance in the wider world. The point here is paying tribute to these extraordinary and diverse performers who have animated and illuminated the aging author's powerful creation. Yet whether the setting is in the minds of moviegoers or the live performances of legendary artists, the phenomenon is still one of cultural recognition. As relationshapers between articulate creators, audiences, and continuing resources, the targeted celebrities have been conduits between one rich source of creativity and another, more general one. In every case of wide regard for their roles, they have made significant personal contributions to established works. Contributions that have been reappraisals and restorations or, as Wilde might phrase it, re-revelations through reinterpretations.

In 1966, Born Yesterday became the fourth movie directed by George Cukor that included iconic Monroe roles. Sixty years before the film's release, critics praised Buckley on the stage. In her zany, confused portrayal, Monroe provided her own unique interpretation of the role, adding a soft sexuality and the warmth created by a simple, straight delivery often free of acting. Without Buckley's All-American sex appeal, Kim Stanley's classroom figure, or Holliday's wide-eyed naivety, Marilyn provided her own unique combination of glistening allure, naïve charm, and knowing determination. Along the path trodden by previous screen stars of Born Yesterday, she appeared to see and queasily regard its perturbations, sense and knowingly grudge its poison, and even grasp and savor its humorous delight, earning for herself star status in the process.

CHAPTER 21

Iconic Fashion and Style

Fashion makes a statement that is there to be noticed, discussed, and, in many cases, envied. The same holds true for style. Fashion is what everyone has ready access to based on financial means and what is part of that season's themes. Style, however, is the result of taking one's personal approach to fashion to another level. Style is doing you and allowing your personality to shine through while helping you define your self-identity choices based on what is available through the commercial fashion world. Fashion is advice from the designer through the department store to the buyer. Style is the result of turning that advice into personal knowledge and expression regardless of whether it fits the season or is even in style.

Iconic models are not necessarily the most glamorous, chic, or fashionable at all times. Instead, they are the individuals other people want to imitate—not just because they are currently the talk of the town—because of something extra. Take, for example, the "little black dress" designed by Coco Chanel. It needs the iconic model who feels at home in the dress and makes it her own in order for her to become the standard for others to want to emulate. Love of clothes or fashion does not promote looking iconic in all apparel, only for particular items, colors, and styles that blend perfectly with the wearer, much in the way Bill Blass did throughout his career and is his still-present legacy. Andrea Lee could spotlight her smooth mahogany skin above the fitted black pants and fine-gauge black T-shirt as she did. No style of sequin gown could hope to duplicate the persona of the woman who wore this and similar creations of her making. Oleg Cassini did not become known for his style by finding First Lady Jacqueline Kennedy's taste. He did it by producing clear single-color lines with a basic classic cut that was her distinctive wardrobe requirement. Women take what a fashion creator offers and personalize it so that it shows who they are and not what they have on. It gives them the same unique style quality that labeled Twiggy, Patricia Neal, or Brigitte Bardot during other periods of time. Women who possess genuine style step away from current fashion trends, look at historical photos, adapt the detail, and then make the next step mirror their person. It's no good leaving it as a generic look. The person—the character they bring to the ensemble—makes it work. André Leon Talley's oversized "Rococo Sun King..." In recent years, Sarah Jessica Parker has thrown down the style gauntlet by calling for women to be less like themselves and more like sex symbols. She is requesting women to stay fresh and original without being permanent museum relics. Her plea is not to copy that looks, just to stay pleased with that inspiration. By asking for the star to be there every day without getting desperate is an enormous requirement of character and consistency. Regardless of their attire at any one time, one can easily spot Diane von Furstenberg, Giorgio Armani, Alber Elbaz, Yves Saint Laurent, or Myriam Ullens as women sporting love, individuality, character, and comfort extended beyond the runway. You can have style when you see the ability to be the person. Iconic consumers have style as the product of their mental endeavors portrayed as a visual presentation of their personality. Otherwise, it is simply a dress, blouse, or tailored pants suit. Balenciaga, Poiret, Schiaparelli, Paul Poiret, and Gianni Versace designed to compliment the individuals who wore them. Ultimate admiration tests the outcome, as this is what people appreciate most looking down Fifth Avenue. Personality cannot be purchased, nor can it be donated. The closest one can come to this mysterious quality is to be yourself, and hope that a bit of it comes out through your charge card.

CHAPTER 22

Iconic Quotes and Catchphrases

"Ayy!" "I'd like to take this opportunity to apologize... to absolutely nobody."

These are a few of our favourite things. Whether you're searching for some extra oomph to pull you through a major event in your own life, or for a mnemonic to remind yourself and others who you are, what you're about, and the kinds of superpowers you bring to the grand table of events that we call life, revisit the amazing one-liners uttered by some of the most celebrated individuals who have ever roamed and endeavoured to shape the rules of this great big world we live in. And when you have achieved the quantum state of being truly iconic, you too will have your own über-cool catchphrase, and a regular drink of water will instantly transform you into an all-singing, all-dancing, human dynamo.

Clothes maketh the man, and slogans doth maketh the brand. After all, there are very few individuals on this planet who do not own and wear clothing that includes the manufacturer's name or logo. Even when we can afford to have our clothing made to measure, we still search for the largest label that we can find in order to emphasize our good fortune. Who wouldn't want the world to know that we are successful enough to hang $2,000 down a thread and strap on the Armani Zoo in the form of a pair of shoes? To improve our status, we need to dress our offspring the same way.

CHAPTER 23

Iconic Roles and Characters

Ricardo Montalbán took part in "Stadfast Tin Soldier," "Mr. Magoo's Christmas Carol," and "Tiger Cruise," but he is known for no role or character more than Khan Noonien Singh of the Star Trek franchise. From the instant he caught the glowing eyes of that Oscar-winning piece of plasticine in 1979, he became Khan, and the idolatry was so all-consuming that his casting as Khan was certain with the anticipation of fans, who knew he had to be playing Khan... as he actually did.

Khan has never appeared in an episode of the Star Trek television series. Iconic though Khan may be, he is the creation of Nicholas Meyer writing a screenplay and of Ricardo Montalbán presenting that screenplay to the world. "It has nothing to do with the few lines I muttered in that episode," Allan Hunt gives for leaving Khan out of William Rostos' book. It is Ricardo Montalbán who has won Khan the iconic classification. That is true because Montalbán recognized the gift and made the most of it: Montalbán remembered the fans and knew that Khan would mean more to them than any role he had played in movies or other television programs. He is a rarity who seemed to be a prince among men. Because of his connection with the short-lived and not much-loved television series, he is not iconographical, he is iconic!

CHAPTER 24

Iconic Performances and Productions

The Library of Congress elected Greer Garson and Angela Lansbury to its Hall of Fame in 1974. The hall exists to give formal recognition to achievements of the most memorable personalities in the industry, recognizing lifetime triumphs in theater, motion pictures, radio, and television. Greer related that she felt wonderful about this acknowledgment, which for her was all of these things. They remain to me today as two of the greatest people I've ever known, just as breathtaking today as when they won our hearts with their award-winning performances. They did not stick out ideologically on the controversial issues that cropped up so often in our time as evolving global citizens. There was a synthesis with their persona and with the attitudes we continue to derive from their magnificent legacy.

Greer (confined by longtime legends) earned nominations for ten major Hollywood movie awards: seven from the Academy, two from the Golden Globes, and one from the British Academy. Angela (whose studio technical skills are extraordinary) has twelve major awards related to her acting: five Tonys, six Golden Globes (winning three), an Olivier, and one of those Academy Award nominations.

Her trophies are well-respected because they reflect the effort she invested, and she has claimed those wonderful accolades built from the solid foundation of her capable skills over time. Thereby, she has earned respect all her life from her devoted audiences, just as Greer did. When Garson was asked about the number of times she said she agreed upon an interpretation of how she played a character, she replied: none. Indeed, you would think that along with Angela (started out in show business from the age of nine), in her seven decades of being in entertainment she must have obtained considerable fame due to her great performances and productions. At ninety-one, she continues performing to her devoted fans by guest starring with aplomb in memorable shows and garnering rave reviews. The lyrics of acclaimed hit songs reveal profound reason to think that every big break that came to them had their own special significance; awards seem to have the unique quality of their own special kind of meaning.

CHAPTER 25

Iconic Songs and Albums

In 1960, the Beatles were considered washed up after several failed auditions with record labels. In 1966, the Rolling Stones might never have appeared on the scene to tell us that time was on our side. Charlie Parker might have gone forgotten had he not picked up the alto saxophone. Ray Charles might not have played the blues. Stevie Wonder might never have been able to "sing a song." The books would not all have been written had Billy Joel not been inspired to say it's nine o'clock on a Saturday. Pop music bears the names of countless artists and timeless melodies that still reverberate through the trite dining rooms of our hearts.

In 1968, Francis Albert Sinatra, Edward Kennedy Ellington, and Ella F. Laine Fitzgerald helped introduce me. With Kate Smith's "God Bless America" reverberating in the background, Rosemary Clooney, the seldom credited mother of George Clooney, served as the quintessential American girl. There's no business like show business, and one of the great rounds of all time was the tournament between Jimmy Durante's schnozzola and Frankie's blue eyes. Although despised by fans who huddle around professors under radar screens, they are enraged by the sight of the F.B.I. Marines buried in grits and canceled their contracts at Capitol Records. When Paul McCartney and Sir Michael McCartney turn 59-length years old,

Capitol will finally release "Villa Del Refugio," the digital recording above all others. Sam Cooke maintained harmonious relationships with his business acts in countless forms. For example, Lionel Hampton is the inspiration for the undying tribute "Night in Tunisia."

CHAPTER 26

Iconic Films and TV Shows

1. TV Show Dr. Ruth (documentary, 2019) A documentary, at 90 minutes, may seem an unorthodox place to build Dr. Ruth's landmark studies and historic public acclaim into some structure. Nevertheless, given her focus on sexual behavior studies and communication, it's particularly sensible even as it avoids the personal aspects of her approach within the particularist framework.

2. Classic Film High Noon (1952) Producer Stanley Kramer tells the story in 90 minutes about an old structure, a classic paradox type where the killer is expected to kill whoever bars him from the town stagecoach. Amidst much anticipation, we eventually see these approaches materialized, and then there are none, the song that dominates this sunrise film.

3. Influential Film The Connectwood (1946) Desperation drives Ralph Kramden, an NYC bus driver in a 39-episode sequence, to operate "my friend the feed". Through its 1950s backdrop of luxurious apartments and China as an increasing income gap, Ralph tries, normally unsuccessfully, to break through the economic and social borders built by the culture of his origins.

4. Classic Film Gentleman's Agreement (1947) With "A Contract with Our Ladies", Gregory Peck's George Peppard portrays another strive for change when he poses as a Jew. He's fired from "Time" and in 90 minutes transforms cancer through his intimate encounters and groundbreaking dialogue with Kathy, his respect for John Garfield's Philip Schuyler Green crime reporter's girlfriend.

5. True-Color Film 12 Edges of Doctor Lao (1964) George Pal explores the intrigue of small-town life, filled with social anxiety generated by one mid-sized movie, The Amazing Stanley (Terry Thomas). What's inside Doctor Lao's tent attracts every member of the Grand Finale, "With 796 exactly what the ad says is what they get, giving this amusement and trade attraction city a misleading sight and remarkable feelings."

6. Television Show Funny Girl, Funny Lady (1968-75) Gypsy's challenge (1962), producer Jack Lemmon (correctly) observes that this disastrous stage actor Fanny Brice film won for a successful musical revue. The "chappo" of the ensemble and the place tributes in a cabaret club show that includes those beautiful "standards. The humor explodes between memorable musical numbers, and it continues, with Topol's role and John Patrick's short trip back to the presentation "MacArthur".

7. Television Show The Yellow Rolls Royce (1964) His clever choice of three diverse acts combined in Walter Wood twin drama presents 85 minutes of enjoyable entertainment. The only real constant are the car engines in this section, "Fred and The Rolls Royce" (1962), which offer so many outdoor adventures and opportunities for all types of character fantasy drawing. The reward is a sleek, nearly novel, gear change and a brief storyline of a fledgling entertainer with, at the end of the day, everything going its way.

CHAPTER 27

Iconic Artistic Collaborations

Iconic artistic collaborations, while rare on the landscape of art and entertainment, are the portals joining genius spirits and sharing co-equally in the ultimate expression of inspiration. Paul McCartney and John Lennon, together and separately, individually enjoyed the wandering minstrels' prestige, deepening themselves ever-deeply into the life and times of the never-never immune from OK Corral conflicts. Tony Curtis and Janet Leigh were screen star discoveries drawn down from American stage and television preciosity. Segovia made the guitar relevant at home and invited throughout the world, elevated by the reputation of His Majesty the King of Spain. Hepburn and Tracy were woefully matched partners in a pitch-perfect duet of dancing variations on the themes of pulls of war passion and personal privacy.

In transformed crowds as art world dreams and street imaginings, Andy Warhol and Jean-Michel Basquiat lucidly made forgivable the unforgiven of self-reclamation phrase "master of none." Streisand and Redford retailed the great individualist American experience in drippings of sex fixed in time and space. Billy Joel is the egocentric Beatles twins reborn, alive in the living room so followers could pay directly for membership in his together-alone embrace discovering one another tongue-operating touchings. King was Broadway re-set to pass one night stands after one-night stands in stardom and recognition. Astaire and Rogers were multi-media dancers performing greater hits like Superball straight to their adoring public around the world. Walt Disney and Mickey Mouse, Goofy, Donald Duck, and the Seven Dwarfs connoisseur are self-aggrandizing laughs.

CHAPTER 28

Iconic Business Ventures

Robert Redford once advised, "I have always been an independent spirit. Publicity is not important to me, nor is an outrageous paycheck if it is going to change the whole tenor of a situation." Redford has always lived by his sage advice, and it has served him well. He founded the Sundance Institute in 1981 - dedicated to furthering the appreciation of film.

Heidi Klum has created a number of very successful business ventures, including a national fashion magazine. She has stated that she thought very hard about this venture before undertaking it.

Madonna has been successful not just in business as a recording artist, film actress and producer, and children's book author, but also as a businesswoman. The book and film writing parts of her career have made so much money for her that in 1992 at a book party in Hollywood, Madonna cheerfully told a reporter, "I know I'm a business, but I like my employees to think of me as a friend." She has also successfully exploited the Madonna brand.

CHAPTER 29

Iconic Awards and Recognitions

Today, most iconic celebrities are often rewarded for their extraordinary achievements. They receive the highest film acting honors with the most prestigious awards in active competition by both the American Film Institute (AFI) and the National Academy of Recording Arts and Sciences (NARAS). They are considered to be the four highest film honors in the United States. Upon winning these awards, recipients are often granted national recognition. Several institutions bestow awards and other accolades for excellence in the field of music. Celebrities receive these awards determining the winners based on their authenticity. Certain awards, however, are unknown to the public but are prestigious within the industry.

Many occupations have a specific degree of coverage that interests the news media. In the United States, film, television, sports, politics, and personal appearances are major parts of the entertainment. Today, celebrities appear on television, feature films, books, newspapers, fashion, and the World Wide Web. Several industries surround celebrities and are the basis for most of their ventures. Iconic celebrities receive many awards for their professional abilities in acting, singing, songwriting, and composing scores for feature films and television. They also receive awards for their business acumen from this specific industry. The following list describes the best-known music awards in the world today. The Music Industry Records' KNKX listed 19 awards for excellent achievements by recording artists.

CHAPTER 30

Iconic Endorsements and Sponsorships

As the years have gone on, brands and teams have left sporting affiliations to celebrities, particularly in the areas of track and field and golf. When these endorsements arrive, what has been interesting to witness is how the methods of the endorsements are changing almost as frequently as the representatives themselves. Gone are the days that a celluloid clip of an individual has any relevance to all but their adoring fans. Hence, the concepts of endorsement and sponsorship have taken over.

Far from being saved for trading purposes by old field sports heroes with only so many caps or VISA sponsored through golf in very rare and selective circles, these specialized and lucrative arrangements are today widespread and perform what they claim to do. Those of us who are not sufficiently inspired to rush out and buy something just because a sporting hero is shown wearing it can but see that there are relationships between sporting professionals and any number of organizations. The organizations give benefits in kind and cash to the sportspeople over and above whatever financial terms their contracts provide, and the sportspeople utilize the organizations in order to afford the accessories and lifestyle their talent demands. It is a two-way street that offers a stark evolutionary change from days previous when successful sports teams and clubs derived the larger part of their business from football pool viewing syndicates underwriting Christmas raffles or the occasional sponsored team blazer designed to hold programme sheets and tabards.

CHAPTER 31

Iconic Social Media Presence

If you were launching a career today, you would make careful choices regarding the best social media platforms to showcase your brand. As a celebrity, you are brands in and of themselves. Do you even need to engage in every platform? Hardly. The trick is to understand who consumes your content and what platforms they prefer. Your goal is to be present where your fan base already hangs out. We are all familiar with large fan bases and how they interact. Vulnerability breeds authenticity, and a legitimate social media network can communicate deep, bonded personality with those in your circle. Each post can literally connect to millions of fans, breaking down barriers to the traditional celebrity/fan relationship.

Your western society nourishes a celebrity-obsessed culture and fosters odd, one-sided photographer/me photographer exchanges. Culture is what fuels the celebrity gravy train, with celebrities serving as ad advocates and walking-talking living endorsements. That all makes social media more influential today than at any time in history. Platforms representing the voice of society have produced literal fortunes for a chosen few. Quite frankly, being emblematic of the culture trend that worships celebrities can be the difference between massive long-term financial wealth and complete obscurity. If the truth be known, few celebrities launched by traditional means were positioned to earn fabulous wealth. Keeping a traditional job is not particularly lucrative, declining social mobility, and high costs for everything have made icon attributes more precious. With those rakish looks adding a tiny dose of edge and socialism, you will greatly expand your market. When you further cultivate your social media urbane cool status, watch out!

CHAPTER 32

Iconic Fan Interactions

"Iconic Fan Interactions" - In which readers declare their love for the celebrities who have transformed their lives and express their gratitude for those mysterious moments of chance when the world's most famous individuals emerged from the bank of clouds in the sky to walk among them for a while, transforming the fans from mere mortals into super beings.

Fan Mail Build-Up - Surveillance And The Stalker Fan - The Intrusive Fan - Fan Crushes - Mob Rule - The Fan Mail/Danger Connection - Fan Potential And The Cult Of Celebrity. The world's most famous individuals are kept aloof from their fans by managers, publicists, and security advisors. They are also encouraged to believe that their fans are as unpredictably dangerous as they are unchangingly loyal. There have been some unfortunate consequences of this attitude. Fandom, a deferential form of dependent entertainment-consumption, is easily discouraged. Now that the Internet has opened up new channels of communication, the relationship between fans and celebrities is changing.

CHAPTER 33

Iconic Charity Events and Initiatives

1) Reach for the stars, and you may come to the ultimate understanding: each of us can do something to make the world a better place. As a United Nations Messenger of Peace, George Clooney has brought attention to several human tragedies, and top chefs from around the world celebrate the city where he walks by hosting a Bring Home the Bacon dinner at the famous Al Lido restaurant on September 13, with proceeds going to victims of the Padua flood. Some celebrities use their talent and influence to organize fundraisers for various causes, including Mariah Carey, Bono, and Elton John in the event known as amfAR's Cinema Against AIDS. Other actors, including Sharon Stone, campaign for vaccines against AIDS for children.

2) A favorite event for gourmet celebrities takes place in Monte Carlo at the World Food Day Gala. Created to generate funds to feed the hungry in twenty-five developing countries, the Gala has attracted several celebrity-cooks for the cause, including Hugh Grant, Karl Lagerfeld, Dame Shirley Bassey, Milla Jovovich, and Britney Spears the year they joined the five hundred VIP guests from business, society, politics, and showbiz. Television actor-turned child ac-

tor advocate Ron Rifkin worked with Jane Goodall, the Duke of Badajoz, and Gina Lollobridgida in support of the Spanish Association for UN in a joint venture with Goodwill in Los Angeles and the participation of Prince Albert of Monaco to benefit the flow of humanitarian supplies to Africa, and astronaut Alan Bean uses his art to raise funds for a museum for disadvantaged kids. With the power behind today's stars, it's easy for them to outshine the sky and the horizon.

CHAPTER 34

Iconic Achievements in Sport

Athletes who can emulate supremely talented actors are few – the Michael Jordans, Muhammad Alis, and Jack Nicks of the world. The nearest equivalents in the world of acting have made both a small handful of classic films and a similar number of personal journeys. These characters have such powerful and charismatic personalities that they have nearly as many fans and admirers who have become inspired or mesmerized by personal feats such as carrying the American flag, being responsible for the most successful children's charity in America, or narrowly avoiding an execution for armed robbery. The journeys of these iconic embodiments of sporting legends would be at home in dramatic narrative, which is probably why actors have secured Academy Awards and Oscar nominations for their performances in sports films.

Elected by the wider public, galvanizers in the sports arena embody the social, gender, and racial transformations that have been the source of achievement and unification of whole cities or countries. These men and women pass into popular mythology because they transcend their sport and the land of their birth in order to redefine the concept of the phenomenal social figure. Their personality fascinates a people eager for the benefit of divine blessings, with the desire to emulate heroes who shape our emotions. The love that they elicit is clearly evident in the widespread sampling of incidents and events concerning the sporting legends within these pages. They combine professional excellence with the highest moral standards in life itself.

CHAPTER 35

Iconic Achievements in Science and Innovation

Watson and Crick, with Maurice Wilkins, the co-recipient of the Nobel Prize, discovered the structure of the DNA molecule. The significance of their work was soon to be realized. The genetic material, designated deoxyribonucleic acid (DNA), which resides in the chromosomes of the cell, is made up of pairs of four nucleotides aimed at transmitting genetic information from one generation to another. The genetic code of all organisms is based on the order of the pairs within the DNA. Because of the molecule's unique capacity to self-replicate, the genetic material is copied whenever a cell divides. Since the molecule continually accumulates errors, new genes are formed. Large quantities of DNA are required for these mutations to be accumulated. The DNA molecule is made up of two intertwined chains which are the complementary sites of one another, in which the nucleotides form each one of the chains and the helix is connected by the pairing of the chains.

Cloning humans would represent an enormous medical achievement. It would necessitate the correction of many defective genes in gene therapy, but we are still not able to direct the way in which DNA, which consists of dozens of nucleotides, determines the eventual genetic characteristic, for which the DNA is responsible. It would necessitate the growth of millions of a particular cell within the nucleus of another, embryonic cell, until a whole human body was formed, but at the present time we still do not have control of a simple living cell. The biological process of fertilization, in humans and in other organisms, can be reproduced in lab experimentation, but scientists still do not understand the biological mechanisms that ensure the correct rearrangement of the genetic materials which two cells transmitted to their offspring, nor can they predict all the characteristics of a future child. Indeed, the story of Huxley's object-grown children has yet to be fulfilled by scientists in a laboratory anywhere in the world.

CHAPTER 36

Iconic Achievements in Politics and Leadership

In many countries, political leaders play a larger part in shaping and documenting society than any other public figures - although they don't call it that. Statecraft is indeed the art of the possible, and building a nation-state is the biggest construction work of all. In some cases, political leaders develop an iconic image by denying icon status to anybody else at a distance greater than 30 feet. Being both instinctive and promiscuous, iconoclasts exist beyond aesthetic debates about art. Arriving late to the party is a common jarring trait. If you weren't traipsing through dead leaves for a while, would you be so keen to pay your respects at lodges and exhibits?

Popular memories of political statesmen cannot be forced. The lean, mean, fast-running father of the nation will not shrivel if his running was more labored than his image. So what was accomplished during the exodus from derailed states so closely associated with the fastest evolution ever witnessed in the historical kingdom of Kama? During brief or ill-conceived stays, adventurers from faraway empires to graveyards fought foes more empty-corporeal or nights-of-the-living dead than actually alive. Terracotta or stoned pacification of pacified provinces is an alluring thought conventionally enforced through the wrong means. Tribal states avoided the later dead-end routes of empires running empires by counting or entering the tribes of others. It also is true that few marvel at the yet-erected real estates of pampered rulers. For lesser-known mentors of distinction, sanctioned contexts may have had more enduring effects than the monuments raised in their honor.

CHAPTER 37

Iconic Achievements in Literature and Writing

Ten years of intense work brought me recognition in the sexual field, which I valued and still value. Even if I had not done anything else, my day would have been rich in possible speed pockets. Just the same, since I was still a woman, I was drawn equally to performance in art, literature, politics, and philosophy. This was much less easy to realize for me at my stage of development, but still the route I chose. The realization of these dreams became possible when I ceased to search for all happiness in woman's love. Then they unfolded their sails in a stormy wind, which life in that splendid way lent me. But my first ten years were not really passed till I had accomplished what Dr. Adler in his "superficial" way had suggested: That I could realize myself completely as such only as a man. Dr. Adler had been right.

I went to analyze with a great friend of Pete's who had a consuming passion for music. She was very sympathetic, and we became warm friends. In 1924, I had the impressive and rare experience of attending the performance of Beethoven's Ninth Symphony at the great hall in Vienna. It was magic and intoxication to be with the big, noble elements of Beethoven despite all language hopelessness, that melts whole pieces so beautifully together that the red flame of joy burns high and powerful and makes us expand and be more beautiful. I also staggered in the dominant chord D flat major rapture I experienced with Ravel's "Rapsodie Espagnole." At the performance of Verdi's "Otello," conducted by Toscanini with great emotion, the pleasure I had experienced at the beginning of the opera had long been lost. I think that I completely broke off the Wander period when I had finished "Twilight of the Gods."

CHAPTER 38

Iconic Achievements in Music and Performing Arts

The fields of music and the performing arts are replete with iconic people, songs, compositions, albums, performances, works, heraldic events, grand noble landscapes, and actions of remarkable valor and uplifting and flawless dignity. Iconic celebrities in these fields have won the hearts and minds of billions of people worldwide, generations of consumers, producers, and connoisseurs alike, from all walks of life, social classes, and from every corner of the planet. And, through exceptional talent, hard work, perseverance, a touch of genius, luck because "talent is luck; the important thing in life is courage", and taking good advantage of opportunities, they have been able to further incredible deeds, exemplify culture, establish standards of excellence, and create beauty that place them on pedestals for eternal contemplation, admiration, and veneration.

Long-lasting associations and passions are created when they perform, and probably this reoccurrence of collective excitement and wonder must provide some explanation to words such as bliss, explosion, and rapture, which are spelled with both "C" and "S". From operatic and symphonic masterpieces to classical, square, and modern dances; from jazz, country, and rock songs to recitals, close harmonies, and extraordinary concertos for piano, violin, and cello to grand symphonic masterpieces like Beethoven's 9th Symphony, where the sounds (no, the voices) of a full choir, four soloists, and an orchestra don't perform their strife, their fears, and their symptoms; they just unite people, calm hearts, and provide healing to all during significant gatherings.

CHAPTER 39

Iconic Achievements in Visual Arts and Design

This section features individuals famous for their exceptional work in the visual arts and design. Review these careers to see how the journeys of the visual masterpieces attract adoration and recognition. The visual artists and designers in this publication are people who, through their individual efforts, singular talents, and incredible vision, have composed, portrayed, constructed, crafted, designed, photographed, and performed visionary works of art. Some have achieved extraordinary and exceptional works. Their footprints in art and photography, both technically and stylistically, are impressively meaningful.

Explore with us and witness their successes to better understand the astonishing skill, depth perception, deep insight, and introspective view they are able to offer the world. While the overall impact resulting from the work of each of these remarkable individuals is vast, at the very core, the philosophy, technology, and grasp of the visual arts and family of concepts at hand cause the greatest of all attributes to emerge and showcase the best the visual artist can ever offer. At the core of this magazine are internationally respected and admired visual artists, including numerous award-winning and humanitarian laureates—all of whom are recognized as visionaries of their respective crafts across a variety of mediums, including photography, painting, 3D digital arts, architecture, design, sculpting, lettering arts, and visual journalism, to mention just a few. Their creations represent more than mere mechanisms of expression. Rather, they embody living and lasting tools for communicating concepts and emotions on a truly universal level. These works have inspired, encouraged, and been highly praised for well over a generation. Histories of the artists and their art, as well as the philosophies, techniques, art forms, and diverse expertise they employ, are as relevant today as they have ever been. Their inspiring stories inspire and pass on visual art to a comprehensive audience.

·

CHAPTER 40

Iconic Achievements in Film and Television

The contributors to this book cover a generous spectrum of careers from various branches of the entertainment industry. Since many of the featured personalities have been equally successful in both film and television, the areas of coverage are frequently overlapping. It seemed a logical approach to concentrate primarily on entertainment careers that have made a wide and visible impact both internationally and nationally. Jack Webb has done exceptionally well in merging movie and television stardom. Martha Ray, Walter Brennan, and Orson Welles have also managed a dual media impact successfully, but Jack Webb has no peer as a television executive producer-star. His professional commitment to deliver commercially to an industry consortium rules his life. Whenever he strikes blows in any direction, there are results. Currently, there is "Dragnet," focusing primarily on blue-collar crime situations, but supplying an ongoing education for disenchanted parents and doubtful teenagers who are trying to understand the shifting frontiers of teenage morality.

Ernst came to television after a first-class career in Hungarian films, where he grew up following his father's death when Ernst Jr.

was nine years old. Magda made her first picture at Lupinos and often played nubile young women, not always successfully due, no doubt, to being subjected to truly unique makeup procedures, like Ida Lupino. Magda, who was thirteen years older than Ida, suffered contumely from resentful Ida co-workers, though Ida was sweet to Magda, who was principally studied and treated as a men's room joke. Ida was production seating her in Texas when it was discovered that Magda was several years before Ida was known on radio, before fame was brought closer to her in the eighties by approaching the occupation which she longed to pursue, using the name "Actress/Director/Producer."

Ron Ely appeared in two Tarzan movies, portrayed the memorable Doc Savage for television, hosted a documentary show for two years, and had many TV series guest shots, including Gary Moore & John Wayne. He made the most out of a busy professional life and during a ten-year association with Miss Kathleen Bennett. She is currently in the apron stage, producing and occasionally directing a top TV show which is performed in South Carolina. The South Carolina skyline slopes sinisterly toward the coast. When fog is thrown in, watch out. Children of all ages will too late understand the real meaning of "Skyfall" from the farewell lyrics by the title song singer near the movie's end. Prevailing weather types did for five fellow characters in "Skyfall," currently an appendage to an extended run of seven productions that hustle eighty-two James Bond crew people to distant points of the globe.

CHAPTER 41

Iconic Achievements in Fashion and Beauty

The world of fashion holds its stars in both the creation and wearing of its designs. The designers create glamour, the models promote them, and the socialites wear them and make them famous. In the ultimate fashion showdown, the celebrities wear them with universal impact. According to fashion experts, some fifty to sixty celebrities really matter in the fashion world - celebrities like Kate Moss, Jean Shrimpton, Twiggy, Iman, Paloma Picasso, Gloria Vanderbilt, Lauren Hutton, Isabella Rossellini, Penélope Tree, and Bianca Jagger, to Simone Gesell, Babe Paley, or Annabeth Gish, who all influenced the fashion world. They epitomize style and pique our icons as they set the highest levels of style and elegance. The (mostly) women of fashion emerge from various fields. There are the models, the sister actress, the socialite who is known for being rich and beautiful, the fashionable writer, and the fashion doyenne.

CHAPTER 42

Iconic Achievements in Business and Entrepreneursh

Achieving business and entrepreneurial success often implies a journey that is arduous, challenging, and fraught with endless risk. Such is the life of the entrepreneur who has achieved that often-elusive goal. The risks are plentiful and complex for today's business leaders: managing growth in a company characterized by innovation, running a globally oriented business in a changeable international economic climate, and skillfully leveraging the success of national and international branding efforts. These iconic businesspeople have achieved success in very different fields and across multiple sectors. At the same time, there are important commonalities that connect them all. These winning entrepreneurs stand out as leaders and much, much more. They've demonstrated singular ability to respond to changing conditions in today's increasingly dynamic business environment and the promise of additional technologies that will continue to change American lives, as they have so many times in the past.

Creating a world-class business is one of the toughest challenges facing a daring entrepreneur. These are winners with nerve and staying power, and their incredible success is testimony to the fact that they're willing to risk substantial wealth to attain their amazing entrepreneurial goals. Classic American industries such as retailing and down-home goods and services can still reward the entrant with uncommon success. This is the dedication and repertoire that produce not simply remarkable profit potential or the pursuit of personal gain, but some of the most iconic business achievements in the country today. Dedicated to innovation and quality, their sense of mission will ultimately result in creating millions of new jobs and billions of dollars in revenue. Yes, these winning business entrepreneurs are truly masters of a modern American success story.

CHAPTER 43

Iconic Achievements in Philanthropy and Social Imp

The remarkable and commendable commitment of celebrities to offering their resources, time, talent, and energy—and sharing of themselves with others who are struggling and are less fortunate—knows no bounds. The enthusiastic support of the public is both present and conspicuous, further signifying that such prominent, influential individuals coming to the aid of others is highly valued. Certainly though, the truest acknowledgment and gratitude come from those whose needs are being met. In the text that follows, we spotlight a few notable celebrities whose philanthropy and efforts to make a social impact and positive change have continued to encourage and inspire, oftentimes noticeably affecting humankind, our planet, and its precious and vulnerable animal inhabitants.

A precedent for several generations following, Marlon Brando used his icon status for social and humanistic change. In the early 1950s, the associate of Dorothy Day's extraordinary Catholic Worker Movement, founding humanitarian Jessica Mitford and her husband, attorney Robert Treuhaft, were brought to Brando's attention; the couple introduced a passion for social justice issues and

GBM organizations to Brando, inspiring the celebrated actor to become involved in a number of charitable, philanthropic, and humane activities over the subsequent years. Sands of Iwo Jima co-star Forrest Tucker suggested the fledgling Marlon Brando Hi-Y Club of the Los Angeles chapter of the YMCA. A close friendship developed between the blacklisted, progressive Treuhaft and the young Brando. Robert Treuhaft provided the future iconic actor with a rudimentary education in basic American history and contemporary issues.